STOP THE STRUGGLE!
Solutions for Parenting Gifted Tweens and Teens

By Margit Crane, M.A., M.S., M.Ed.

©2009 All Rights Reserved

STOP THE STRUGGLE!
Solutions for parenting gifted tweens and teens

No part of this publication may be reproduced, stored in a retrieval system, or transmitted in any form or by any means, electronic, mechanical, photocopying, recording or otherwise, without prior permission of the author.

Copyright © Margit Crane
1st Edition, 2008
2nd Edition, 2009
All Rights Reserved
U.S.A.

Disclaimer
The techniques described and the advice given in this book represent the opinions and experiences of the author. The author is not licensed to practice medicine and therefore expressly disclaims any responsibility for any liability, loss or risk, personal or otherwise, which is incurred as a result of using any of the techniques or recommendations suggested herein. If in any doubt, or if requiring medical advice, please contact the appropriate health professional.

ACKNOWLEDGEMENTS

To my parents, Jean & Sol Roshal: Thank you for always doing your best.

To my teachers (and there were many!): Thank you for inspiring me to be the best Margit I could possibly be. Bless you and your often unsung efforts.

To my coaches - Dan, Jean-Pierre, Laura, Miriam, Sandi, and Betsy: Thank you for your amazing wisdom. You are all so fun!

To my clients: Thank you for sharing your lives with me. It is such an honor to serve you.

To my friends: I'm one-dimensional without you. Thank you for playing full out. I adore you all.

To my step-kids, Mike and Nichole: I am so lucky to be your stepmother and I love you a lot. Thanks for accepting me from day one.

To my best friend and husband, Nick: You are, quite simply, the best thing that ever happened to me. Thank you for believing in me and for making me laugh so much.

And last, but CERTAINLY not least...

To God/the Universe/Spirit/Higher Power: Thank you for everything you've given me and for everything you've taken away.

TABLE OF CONTENTS

Introduction, p9

You are here, p13
1. What's going on?
2. Does my teen really hate me?
3. The good-enough parent
4. I haven't done my best
5. How do I start over?

Rules & consequences, p22
6. How much independence?
7. How do I create rules?
8. What if my teen grumbles?
9. Feeling guilty
10. No consequences?
11. "Fitting the crime"
12. Nothing left to take away
13. When do we have fun?

Teens & emotions, p31
14. Trusting my teen
15. Teen acting out
16. Pushy teens
17. I get angry too
18. The teen brain
19. TV and video games
20. Teen with mood swings

Different types of teens, p40
21. Bossy teens
22. Aggressive teens
23. Needy or clingy teens
24. Shocking teens
25. Stubborn teens
26. Dishonest teens

Teens at school, p46
27. Lazy teens
28. Gifted with low grades
29. AD/HD teens
30. Cliques
31. Bullying
32. The teacher hates my child

Teens & relationships, p54
33. Popularity
34. Peer Pressure
35. Gifted and immature
36. Abusive relationships
37. Teens and sex
38. Too much information!

New partner, new marriage, p61
39. I'm dating again
40. Betrayed!
41. Here come the bride & groom
42. Preparing for a new stepparent
43. 5 tips for new stepparents
44. Co-parenting
45. One child not adjusting

Conclusion, p69

About Margit, p71

INTRODUCTION

WELCOME! And KUDOS for taking the first step to resolving your parenting struggle.

I have been offering presentations and workshops to parents, stepparents and guardians of gifted tweens and teens for several years now. This book was inspired by the brave and devoted parents, like you, who come for workable solutions to their family frustrations and their personal pain.

Do you have a tween or teen who is underachieving, over-irritating, or both? How can this be? Doesn't "gifted" imply maturity, responsibility, and high achievement? Even if our kids are dealing with family divorce, social immaturity, AD/HD or other challenges, shouldn't the "gifted" label override these bumps in the road? If only it were so, but this is precisely where we, as parents, are misled; giftedness and emotional maturity do not correlate. It is rare indeed to meet the teen who is gifted emotionally, regardless of what THEY may think!

Suffice it to say that "intelligence" is a complex concept and, depending on whether your child is gifted academically, musically, in sports or in some other area, those gifts can be strengthened or blocked depending on the level of development and the smooth functioning of the brain's emotional center, the limbic system.

Thus, one of the main struggles for families with gifted children is reconciling the gift with relative emotional immaturity. It is so thrilling to be told that your child is gifted and that thrill inspires us to provide whatever experiences will enhance this gift. What is common, however, is that we parents lose sight of the whole child, focusing on that part that gives us such pride and enjoyment.

This is a natural tendency, yet it contributes to our confusion and frustration: How can a teen be gifted and yet be so stubborn, rude, and lazy? For answers, let's look at another natural tendency – that of the gifted child:

When people are labeled they may feel relief but more often they feel pressure to live up to the label or to live it down. Many children, when told they are gifted, are confused by what this means for their present lives, and what it may mean in the future. It sounds exciting, but they wonder what "being gifted" may require of them. Remember that children don't really have the depth to look holistically and impartially at a concept which holds such emotional weight.

Some children rise to the occasion but others, particularly with the onset of puberty, rebel out of fear and the enormity of perceived expectations. The fact that their brains are rebuilding themselves at this time in their lives just adds to the load. Anxiety and self-obsession set in. Underachievement, emotional isolation, and/or rudeness and angry outbursts become coping mechanisms. Gone is the cuddly infant you fell in love with. Instead, you're living with a prickly porcupine that has an answer for everything!

Do any of these sound familiar?

- ✓ My friends don't care if I get A's, why should you?
- ✓ It's the teacher's fault.
- ✓ This class is too hard. Ask anyone.
- ✓ I'm okay with getting B's and C's. That's still above average.
- ✓ I have a game/recital/lesson. I don't have time to study.
- ✓ Can you bring my project to school? Uh, I don't know where I left it.
- ✓ I did my homework in school.
- ✓ Nothing.
- ✓ Maybe.
- ✓ Later.
- ✓ I don't remember.
- ✓ LEAVE ME ALONE!
- ✓ I'm getting all A's! You have nothing to complain about!
- ✓ I'll be on my own in 3 years – I'm practically an adult!
- ✓ You SUCK! I hate you both!

Surprisingly, gifted teens need as much (if not more) attention, support, and understanding as their less gifted counterparts. They have little idea of how to successfully engage with the world as adults but they are all too aware of what is expected of "the gifted student." Thus their teenage years are fraught with anticipatory anxiety. By ignoring their very basic needs we teach them avoidance, fear, judgment, and anger. When we agree to guide them we teach love and compassion and hope and triumph and joy.

And that's where I step in – having lived the life of an underachieving, over-irritating gifted child myself, having taught gifted children, having step-parented two, and now working with them in my practice, I am very familiar with the front lines, and work with clients to develop and implement family structures that support each particular family's values, beliefs, desires, and needs.

It is my privilege and joy to demystify teens for their parents, and parents for their teens. I trust that this book will be a first step for parents of gifted children who want to repair (or prepare for) their relationship with their teens.

At your service,

Note: In most cases, the words "kid" "child" "tween" and "teen" are used interchangeably.

chapter one
You are here

#1 - What is happening to my sweet child? Overnight he/she turned moody and angry. Nothing I do is right. I miss my angel.

When I was doing teacher training, a very wise professor taught me his three rules for success that I believe apply to parenting also:

1) Some things are inevitable.
2) Don't take things personally.
3) You may never know the effect you've had on your students (or children).

To answer your question, let's look at Rule No. 1.

Remember that it is normal and appropriate for your teens, gifted or not, to practice testing their boundaries (and testing you along with it!). In order for them to grow into healthy adults they must "individuate," which means just what it sounds like: they must become individuals. This has been happening, slowly, ever since the umbilical cord was cut. The big push happens during adolescence, partly because of physical changes that affect their emotions (more about that in Chapter Three).

The other part is that we, as a society, value adults who are not enmeshed with their parents. We look askance at the thirty-year-old who still lives with mom and dad. Our society believes that a psychologically healthy adult has an individual personality, with personal preferences and the ability to make those known. We like people who know what they want and go out and get it!

Why is this important? Because when we agree with a belief we do our utmost to uphold our convictions. This means that you, the Parent, has actually been hoping for this new behavior, albeit unconsciously, to *confirm* that your child is on his or her way to becoming an adult.

So then, congratulations! The inevitable has happened, thank goodness, and now the trick is to celebrate these changes and to move forward as the parent of a baby adult. Read on!

#2 – I feel like my teen hates me. What do I do?

Let's look at the second rule above: **Don't take things personally**.

Your teen is going through a lot of emotional upheaval; that's the inevitable part. Some teens handle it better than others - often depending on how sensitive they are - and gifted teens are often more sensitive than other teens. Think of your teen as a toddler-adult, ready to take off but without sufficient life skills. They are encountering adult emotions, adult expectations from others, their own adult dreams, early adult body chemistry, adult triumphs, and adult disappointments.

When your tweens and teens were toddlers, they too were often frustrated and would throw tantrums for lack of a better way to express their needs and their emotions. Your teen may also throw tantrums in the face of challenges that he/she has no clue how to handle. The sulking, the "eye-daggers," the shouting, the slamming doors, and the isolation are all versions of a Teen Tantrum and you do not need to take it personally. **These episodes indicate that your toddler-adult is up against something that he or**

she does not understand and, whether your child asks for your help or not, help is what he or she would like. Now they might not want YOUR help... They might want the help of another adult and, hopefully, there are some trustworthy ones that your teen can turn to.

Note, however, that if these behaviors are fairly constant or if they persist for more than 6 months, even though you have learned how to talk to your child about what's going on, it is probably time for professional help!

#3 – How do I know if I'm a good enough parent?

That brings us to the third rule: **You may never know the effect you've had...**

Now this is not quite the same for parents as it is for teachers. Presumably you are going to be a participant in your child's life for quite a long time. But that's not the thrust of the rule...

What this rule addresses is that:

1) We need to develop a core of integrity that informs our parenting;
2) We can't base our parenting decisions on whether or not we see the results that we want; and
3) Waiting for, hoping for, or expecting thanks for all the hard work you do is a setup for disappointment. We must take on the responsibilities of effective parenting simply because we have chosen to parent!

Now the cool thing is that in most cases, because you are willing to maintain your integrity as a parent, you DO see the hoped-for results and you DO receive the gratitude of your kids. But you can't do it for that reason. You do it because you want the very best for your children.

Consult an outsider whom you can trust. This will give you the perspective on which to base a self-assessment. Remember that your children are individuals and how they turn out is not simply based on your parenting skills. On the other hand, ask yourself,

- Am I doing the best that I can at this moment?
- Am I making our home a safe environment?
- Am I teaching my children the skills to function as successful adults?

The honest answers will make themselves known.

#4 – I've blown it. I know I haven't done my best as a parent. Now what?

First of all, congratulations on owning up to your mistakes! Already that makes you a winner!

I'm not sure how you know you've "blown it" but let's go with two possibilities:

1) Your teen is getting into trouble or is unhappy, or
2) You are aware that you've made some unhealthy choices and you want to remedy that.

Let's start with the first case. Please keep in mind that kids do make their own decisions quite often! Especially with teens, those decisions are the result of being ill prepared to handle a particular scenario. So your job, whether or not you deem this to be "your fault," is to start over.

This happens quite often with parents I meet. **We assume that when children hit their teens they should be able to handle more freedom and more responsibility. This is often not the case at all.** Despite what they might be telling you about being "almost an adult" they are, in many cases, much closer to childhood than adulthood. So when we've given them too much freedom or too much responsibility *(you'll know by the increase in rather "UN-adult" behavior or the decrease in agreeable family moments),* it's time to rein them in.

Sorry about the horse analogy... My mother often quoted Robert Frost who wrote, "Freedom is riding easy in the reins." I love that quote. The idea is that people need
structure in order to know true freedom. All children need rules to make sense of their world. And in understanding their world, there is freedom. (We're going to talk more about that in the next section: **Rules and Consequences**). The answer, then, has two parts:

1) create new structures for your family; and
2) communicate them effectively to your kids.

More about that in a second...

On to the second possibility: If you have made some unhealthy choices regarding your own life and this has affected your parenting, you're in luck! You, too, can start again. **In fact, the skill set that it takes to admit your mistakes—willingness, honesty, self-reflection, and humility—are precisely the skills you need to cultivate to be a truly great parent!** So you're on your way!

I believe in The Heartfelt Apology (and it scores big points with teens, who are all about integrity). Here's my version:

> **I want to apologize to you. I haven't been the parent that you deserve. I've been afraid that you wouldn't like me so I've made decisions that really aren't the best for our family. I want you to know that it is my intention to change my behavior and to be a parent you can trust. That means there will be changes in our family. We will have healthier interactions so that you can become the kind of person that you can be proud of. I hope that you will forgive me but if you don't I'm OK with that. I love you very much and I always will.**

That's the basic version; you can adapt it to your situation. What's important is that
you convey that your decisions from now on will be based on what's best for the health of the family and for your kids' futures.

Will there be resistance? Absolutely! (Well, probably). And it will come from you as well as from your family. Your family is a system that has been functioning smoothly (even in dysfunction) for quite some time. You all know how to dance around everyone else's "stuff." Now that you're overlaying a new system, there will be rough patches. The key is not to waver. You are on a Hero's Journey. Remember, you are saving the life of your family. (For more on the Hero's Journey, head to this book's CONCLUSION)

#5 – I've apologized. Now how do I start over?

First of all, resolve to be the parent. There are basically three types of parents, only one of which is actually doing any parenting!

The first type is the **AUTHORITARIAN**, who wants respect more than anything else. This parent is more concerned with appearances, reputation and authority. They believe that being disciplined and learning self-discipline is THE key to success. In order to teach respect the disciplinarian will often resort to verbal and/or physical abuse. "What is wrong with you?" "You are lazy!" "I am ashamed of you!" Their children may withdraw or become bullies themselves.

The second type is the **FRIEND** or **INDULGENT PARENT**. Very often these parents grew up with authoritarian parents and don't want to repeat that mistake. Afraid to lose their children's love (as their parents did) they are reluctant to create and enforce any family standards. Unfortunately, their children may become indifferent or appear lazy. They may also become angry or act out, actually *hoping for a consequence or punishment.*

Or they may become overachievers; in order to compensate for the lack of structure, they structure themselves, **taking on the role of the parent since the parent is reluctant to do so.**

Notice that in neither case is the child allowed to be a child. In the first model, children are expected to adhere to adult levels of self-control. In the second, children are asked to take on the role of best friend to an adult. In the first, there seem to be two adults and in the second, two children. And, ironically, BOTH types of parents can be overprotective *or* negligent!

Actually, the most effective parenting takes the best aspects from each. I call this third type of parent the **INTEGRATED PARENT** meaning they have integrated or melded the concept of discipline or structure with the concept of independence and trust.

Here are the behaviors that, when practiced consistently, make us **Integrated Parents** (that is, *effective parents.*)

1) **Be self-reflective**. When we regularly review our own behavior, our teens see us as more trustworthy.

2) **Honor your kids' individuality** Your child has something unique to offer the world. It may be his or her most obvious gift or it may be something completely different. You get to go on a treasure hunt to discover just what that is!

3) **Take care of your health**. We teach our kids how to treat us (and, by extension, we teach them how to treat themselves) by practicing self-care.

4) **Surround your kids with trustworthy adults**. The more adults they have to look to for support and comfort, the more likely they are to embrace their own growth and impending adulthood.

5) **Refrain from any verbal (or physical) abuse**. Watch how often you put *yourself* down! Our kids are listening!

6) **Spend time listening to your kids**. A child who is not heard will "go invisible," will act out so that you are sure to hear him/her, or will find **anyone they can** who will listen. All are scary to think about.

7) **Talk to them about your life**. Tell them about your triumphs and (some of the more palatable) failures. Above all, focus on how you took steps to reach your goals, how you resolved the disappointments and how you surmounted the challenges.

8) **Don't be overprotective**. When we do for our kids what they can (with some effort) do for themselves, we are telling them, "You're probably not capable of doing this so I'll do it for you." Ouch!

9) **Teach them about feelings**. The more we notice that feelings come and go, the easier it is to feel them fully and move on.

10) **Let your children know that you love them unconditionally** It is possible to be angry at your teen's behavior and still love them deeply... but kids don't know that! Remember that their experience with mature emotion is limited and they need to be reminded that you love them.

chapter two
Rules & consequences

#6 – How much independence should I give my teen?

Just because a gifted child becomes a gifted teen does not mean that all the rules need to be changed to accommodate him or her. In fact, I wouldn't change many of them. What has really changed? Their school schedule and perhaps the schedule of their extra-curricular activities. That doesn't mean that they are able to handle the freedom that comes with altering the family rules.

Sometimes when kids hit middle school a mom will go back to work full-time and isn't around as much to keep an eye on her teens. That is plenty of freedom right there! No need to change much more! For young people big changes mean a bigger need to know where the boundaries are.

How much independence should you give a teen? Not much—they've only aged one year, after all! Whatever your teen says about being "practically an adult," you know that's not true. They need to prove that they can handle the freedom they have asked for. If they haven't proved it to you, why would you give it to them? That's a recipe for disaster! Give them a little at a time and see how they handle it. Also, don't be afraid to "back-track" if it turns out that they actually *can't* handle that much freedom. It's OK; you didn't do anything wrong. Parenting teens is often about trial and error *and trial and success!*

If you want to create a relatively conflict-free home, firmness is KEY. Being firm isn't the same as being mean, although with their as-yet-developing vocabulary and emotional range, that may be how your teen describes it. When you have clear rules and your consequences are reasonable (as opposed to extreme) and are employed consistently and in a matter-of-fact manner, you won't have a lot of conflict.

#7 – How do I create rules that teens will follow?

The answer to this question has several steps to it. As well, it requires trial and error and so I usually recommend working with someone over time to figure out what works for your family. But I don't want to ignore the question as it is totally legitimate.

I have two methods that I use: **The Long Wild List** or **the Values-Based Approach**. Neither is better than the other. Actually, which you use is dependent on your family's personality and on how out of control things are.

The Long, Wild List is compiled by the parents. You write down as many rules as you can think of that would make you feel better. They can be as wild and as crazy as you want since it's not a final list. (You can even write, "You always bow and kiss my feet when I appear," or "You raise your hand when we're at the dinner table and you want to speak.")

Once you have your list (and released a bunch of tension!), you pare it down to the essentials. I usually suggest having the number of rules equal the age of your teen, but that depends on how involved your rules are. Also, most rules fit into categories like "Cleaning up after yourself" or "Going out with friends or dates." So you may have four or five categories with 2 – 4 rules per category.

With the Values-Based Approach, you make a list of your Top 10 Family Values. Then you narrow it down to five, then three. The way you narrow it down is to figure out which rules would correspond to which values AND whether you could follow those rules yourself and whether you could uphold them with consequences if the rules were broken. These are **the key elements**.

For instance, you may value Community and Global Involvement but do you want to, for instance, take away your son's car if he doesn't want to work in the soup kitchen?
Are you willing to attach rules and consequences to this value? If not then take it out of your top three. It doesn't mean this isn't a value for you; it just means that it's not a part of your family rules.

Likewise, some values clash. You can value truth telling and manners but what if one threatens the other? What if your daughter has been sent home from school because she suggested that her teacher might benefit from professional counseling?

This technique takes more thought than the other but it also works.

#8 – What if my teen grumbles about my rules?

That's a pretty safe bet! We hate to hear resistance. Why can't they keep it to themselves? Wouldn't it be great if our kids responded to our rules and consequences by saying, "OK, Mom, I love you." That's my dream!! I want everybody to meet all my suggestions with a "Wow! What a great idea!" I'm not kidding – that's my dream. But that isn't very realistic…

Here's a simple answer that should alleviate some of the pain: when they grumble, assume that it's "teen talk" for "OK, I heard you," and nothing more. It'll take the sting out. Oh, and don't respond defensively or take back whatever you have just told them. Believe it or not, that will only *dis*empower them. Simply say "Thank you," and smile.

#9 – What do I do about feeling guilty about enforcing consequences?

Were you raised by an Authoritarian Parent? Do you feel that because your parent(s) was strict—and you suffered for it—you don't want your kids to have to go through the same thing?

It's pretty common for parents to misgauge what is appropriate, for fear of being too strict. Then they end up giving their children too much freedom.

Also, teens are good at pushing our buttons, and gifted teens are GIFTED at it! But think of it this way: if parents aren't the ones teaching the kids how to be successful adults, who will? And doesn't our whole social structure function with rules and consequences? **Be the kind of adult that you hope they will become.**

You will inevitably encounter some resistance from your kids but understand that YOU may also feel resistant. That's normal. Just stick with it. If I knew that I could get my way by whining incessantly, I would certainly make whining a daily activity! If you stop reacting, they will stop the behavior that used to elicit the reaction. It may take some time, but it will be SO worth it. You are championing your family by setting up rules and consequences. Stay the course and you will succeed!

#10 – What if there are *no* consequences?

To be succinct, if there are no consequences, your children will not be prepared for living as adults in our society. Our world functions because we have boundaries that define acceptable behavior and we have consequences for unacceptable behavior. We may disagree with the rules and we may, at times, get away with ignoring them but on the whole this is a tacit agreement that we make as we become adults. Actions have consequences. It's basic to our world.

Here are some other reasons why it is ***imperative*** to follow through with consequences:

- ❖ It makes no sense to have rules and not consequences. That invalidates your credibility, which you earn by wisely choosing and upholding the behaviors that match your family's values. You devalue your whole family.

- ❖ Having boundaries keeps children safe and actually helps them *feel* safe. Not having consequences thus tells your children that their safety is not very important to you. Upholding their trust in you teaches them that they can trust the world.

- ❖ Setting limits and following through with appropriate consequences teaches children how to interact effectively and safely with others. All you have to do is look at the downward spiral that characterizes the lives of some of our more visible young celebrities to understand just how important this point is.

#11 – Shouldn't the consequences fit "the crime"?

Most of the time this is the way to go. If your child stays out late, impose an earlier curfew. If your teen makes too many cell phone calls, create a consequence that has to do with the cell phone. Most of the time this works perfectly.

There are, unfortunately, times when we need to go further with our consequences and take away a privilege that really means something to our child. For example, if our teen is not capable of meeting the curfew, we may decide to "ground" him or her. Or, we may decide that our child can't hang out with those particular friends. Or, we may send him or her to rehab, depending on the circumstance.

It's really important that we consider each case individually and then figure out what works best for your child in the context of your family. Trying to make each consequence fit is exhausting and often achieves little.

#12 – What if I run out of things to take away?

It's hard for me to imagine that in the average family in North America or Europe you would run out of things to take away. It sometimes becomes very difficult, even painful, to take away something whose disappearance will create anger, tears, more drama, and more tension, but there is always something to take away, including the privilege of living at home.

This is the painful stuff, I know. Don't fret a lot about taking away material things or social opportunities. These are minor compared to what could happen if your children are able to convince you to just give up and let them have their way.

#13 – If I'm always giving my kids consequences, when do we have fun?

This is a really good question. I know it speaks to the heart of some parents' reluctance to uphold consequences. There are several steps to the process of creating appropriate boundaries or rules and effective consequences and this may make it easier for you to incorporate them into your home.

> a) Remember "The Apology" (Chapter One, #4). As an adult you are an empowered member of your family. Your kids are only empowered insofar as you empower them. The idea of "empowering" is not to give away your own power; it is to build your children's self-esteem. By apologizing you tell your kids that you are capable of self-reflection (which they LOVE to see), that you are working as part of a team to be a great parent, and that you are reasserting your role as the nurturer and protector of your family.
>
> b) Have a discussion with your teens and be prepared to LISTEN! I call this **Fearless Listening**. (Listening to them doesn't mean obeying them!) Here are the components of **Fearless Listening: It is non-judgmental, non-correcting, all-accepting and loving.** What does this mean? We know that what our teens have to say isn't always pleasant and can even be hostile. So

it is definitely a feat of willpower, tolerance, and patience to listen fearlessly.

This doesn't mean that you agree with everything that they say. It does mean that you don't need to take it personally. Remember that if you are being triggered by your kids, that's *yours* to resolve. They are just acting out their fears and anxieties about not knowing just who they are and where they stand in the family or the world.

c) *Should you negotiate your rules and consequences with your children?* This question does not have a pat answer. You are recreating the harmony that once existed in your family—that is primarily your job. You get to look at the values that you want to impart to your kids and then figure out which rules will uphold those values. Check with other parents and find out what they do. Take some time and come up with a list of 8–15 rules.

If you would like to offer your teens some say in these rules, consider letting them select 3 of those rules that they would like to alter (like lights out at 1 AM on weekends instead of 11 PM, or they only have to do homework 5 nights a week—it really depends on your family) then you choose ONE of the three that you are willing to alter. If altering all three seems fair and comfortable for you as the parent, go ahead.

Present this as a contract ***and have them sign it;*** that way when they get off track you can always say, "You know the rules. You signed the contract. No arguing." Remember to say it calmly!!

d) Above all, don't start something that you can't follow through on. You don't need to feel defeated yet again! Remember, your boundaries, rules, and consequences ultimately give your children a sense of security, which is invaluable. **Now go have fun!** ☺

chapter three
Teens & emotions

#14 – How can I learn to trust my teens? My son/daughter is always accusing me of not trusting him/her. That makes me feel terrible but the truth is—I don't. Then I feel guilty.

As for trusting your teens, that is a dream we all have. In some families it works. Their teens are trustworthy. However, trusting your teens doesn't make them trustworthy. And being gifted doesn't make them trustworthy either. (Darn!)

The truth is: **It is more important for your teens to trust you than for you to trust them.** They're still kids after all. What do they want you to trust? That they'll be responsible with the car? How can they guarantee that? There is so much that is beyond their control when they are driving. And this applies to other scenarios as well. Being trustworthy is so much more than not telling lies or returning home before curfew. Remember, their emotional range is still limited, their experience scant, and their lives are at stake—don't be coaxed into trusting too quickly.

Trust evolves. I'm sure you trust your teens to a certain extent. It may be time for you to allow them a small opportunity to prove their trustworthiness. If that works, try it again… a little bit at a time. If you have done this and they have violated your trust then back up a bit. Now it's time for them to earn your trust back. They can't control who trusts them but they can control whether or not they engage in trustworthy behavior.

Trust is sacred; it's not something you offer easily like a piece of candy or a new video game for being good.

For more information about how to be a trustworthy adult, visit www.TheGiftedTeenCoach.com. Go to the Teen section and download the free PDF document titled, **Is Anybody Listening?**

#15 - Why do teens act out so much?

Think back to when your kids were newly born. There were times when they cried and cried and cried and you tried everything but just couldn't get them to stop crying. And then you tried swaddling the baby and he/she calmed down and stopped crying. What you did was create a cocoon for your baby—a structure within which he or she could feel safe and soothed.

When your children were toddlers they probably had what's now called a meltdown. Back then it was called a tantrum. You tried everything you could think of to get them to stop screaming. Often what worked was holding them or putting them in their bedroom. Again, you created a cocoon but notice that the parameters are wider for the toddler than for the newborn.

When teens have a meltdown it's usually scarier for parents because they have big bodies and they can think for themselves. It can be more frustrating and more irritating because you're no longer dealing with a usually snuggly munchkin who has simply hit the wall.

But the reasons for the tantrum are similar: your teens have also hit a wall – they have been presented with something (a feeling, a rule, a reaction) that they cannot process with their as yet young and relatively limited emotional range. Isn't that what's happening with your newborn and toddler? They act angry because they don't have to skills to express what is really going on—confusion, frustration, disappointment, guilt, shame—nor do they have adequate skills to deal with these subtle states. Anger becomes the default response.

So the remedy is similar: provide them with a cocoon in which they can feel safe, and that starts at home. Obviously the cocoon needs to be bigger. That's where your rules and consequences come into play. When they are upheld, your teens can trust their immediate world. When we are unwilling, too overwrought, or too tired to stick to our principles **we unsettle our kids even more.**

To be citizens of the world we are expected to follow rules and accept consequences. As "citizens" in our family we also adhere to norms and rules, if you will. Your teen expects this! It creates a sense of belonging that teens, especially, **yearn** for. If we don't provide the cocoon, **they will find one somewhere else.** You have seen the news and you know the lengths that teens will go to in order to feel like they belong to a cause or a group or an ideal.

Make that cause, group, or ideal your family.

#16 – How do I get my teens to stop pushing and pushing? When they're not pushing, they're giving me attitude. I can't stand it. I know I shouldn't let them get to me but I'm too tired to resist.

It is deeply painful to have our babies grow up to be snarling teens. It feels shameful and sad and overwhelming. Know that your teens are feeling something similar.

You know how when you push your teens you're often doing it because they're not living up to their potential? It's pretty much the same with teens pushing you. What does that mean? They want more parenting! I know that sounds fairly impossible, but it's true! Every time they have one of their "episodes," whether it be starting an argument, having a tantrum, or just vanishing to who knows where, be assured that you have the power to heal them. It may take some time and some trial and error. It may mean that you must get some professional help to support your intentions. As painful as it is for you, it is more so for them. Most "uncivilized behavior" comes from confusion and frustration about that confusion. If you are clear about who you are as a parent, and you communicate this effectively, you will erase the confusion.

Here's a step-by-step approach for becoming the parent you want to be. Start at the first step you haven't tried yet:

1. Talk to other parents of teens to find out how they handle these situations. As parents, we tend to isolate out of shame or guilt. The best thing you can do is to compare notes. If you can get a regular support group going, that's even better.

2. If you have a spouse, even if he/she is an ex or a stepparent to your kids, come together to create a workable solution. Bring in observations from school staff and information that you've gathered from other parents. United parenting is POWERFUL!

3. Give them consequences for continuing the attitude and the pushing.

4. Make sure that you are taking care of your emotional and physical health.

5. Believe that you and your family can thrive.

6. Be patient. (I know – easier said than done...)

7. Review these questions & answers. One will be perfect for you.

#17 – When my teens get angry I get angry. My first thought is "@*%# you! How dare you get angry with me? I'm your parent! I don't need this!" I know this is a pointless response. How do I get over my anger?

Thanks for telling it like it is! You are not alone here. I definitely know how easy it is to fall right into that anger vortex. In my early years as a teacher I fell into it many times! I think most people make mistakes when newly faced with an angry teen.

When you are with an angry teen and you get angry, two things happen. First, they think, "Hah! I've got them! I've won!" And second, "What? This is my parent/teacher/coach! They're supposed to know how to hold it together!" Then the third thing happens: you've created a lose-lose situation. The teen realizes that he/she is trapped; there is no way out because you, the adult, would have to be the guide but you're lost, too!

This shouldn't be a competition—you're the parent: YOU WIN! So it's up to you to take a step back and respond calmly. If you are calm without being smug or patronizing or sarcastic (which are all forms of anger anyway) they will calm down - maybe not right away, but remember that you are re-educating your family at this point. When you are calm and confident in your parenting your kids are soothed.

#18 – What's the hoopla about "The Teen Brain"?

If you remember this answer, then every other thing I say will make perfect sense!

The Brain Research (the nutshell version):

The Teen Brain goes through a restructuring process, starting around age 11 for girls or age 12 for boys. The *peak* of this process occurs around age 16. The entire restructuring ends by age 25. (Yes, 25!)

So while you're thinking, "Ahhhh...now he's 12. I can give him more freedom," his brain is screaming, "Help! What's happening to me?" (OK, not really, but do you get my point? This is probably the worst time to make big changes!)

Still not convinced? Well listen to this: The restructuring proceeds from the back of the brain to the front, ending with the stabilization of the PRE-FRONTAL CORTEX (remember that the peak of the restructuring is about age 16; the stabilization comes in their 20s!) The pre-frontal cortex regulates what are called "Executive Functions." These are the nuts-and-bolts of making thoughtful, powerful decisions: Planning, Organization, Goal-Setting, Setting Priorities, Suppressing Impulses, and Weighing the Consequences of Ones' Actions—***all the processes that most challenge teens!***

Now *on top of that* we've got the whole hormonal surge! So here's **Hormones,** in another nutshell: the important thing to know is that the part of the brain that is "assaulted" by the hormonal shifts is the Limbic System, which is the brain's emotional center. When there is a chemical surge (and these occur randomly, as I'm sure you've discovered), teens get a ***charge*** or a ***high***. Then, like addicts, they seek to re-stimulate the region and recreate that charge or high.

They learn quickly that *certain behaviors* act as stimuli: falling in love, obsessing over unrequited love, **getting angry,** and risky behaviors such as drinking, drugging, and smoking (you've got the high from the chemicals and the high from "being cool"). Texting can also produce a high—it's a fast-paced activity with the thrill of waiting for a response. Sadly and horribly, secret rendezvous with friends AND WITH STRANGERS can also replicate the hormone high.

Honestly, this is not the time to abdicate parental authority. I'm sure you see that clearly.

For more information, *Time* and *Scientific American* have published excellent articles that you can find online.

#19 – One of my children is shy, the other is boisterous. What gives?

One thing I've noticed is that when you have a large family it's assumed that your children will be different from one another. When we only have two kids, the differences are striking and it seems puzzling.

Your descriptions of your children suggest that one may be an **introvert** and the other an **extrovert**. Giftedness doesn't correlate with either, and neither is better than the other. These terms don't describe social maturity; they simply describe the manner in which people renew themselves.

Think about some of the people you know (think about yourself!): Some seem a bit anxious or get quiet when around crowds for extended periods of time. They hear noise instead of conversation. Being alone helps them regroup. Some people, on the other hand, just drag around until they get with a group of people. All of a sudden their energy returns! Notice when your children act out and this may clue you in to their temperaments.

Introverts are not necessarily unsocial. If your teen has trouble making or keeping friends, you will probably want to teach him/her some skills such as **small talk, phone/email etiquette, how to pay and receive compliments**, and **how to play to his/her strengths.**

I had a client who was a very shy young man. He wanted to have more friends but didn't know how to accomplish that. We talked about his strengths and he realized that he was a nice person and a good listener. I coached him over the course of a couple months to practice joining in with a group of kids as a *listener* and a "kind commenter." People (especially girls) grew to enjoy his company because he was trustworthy. They valued him as an easygoing, flexible, undemanding addition to their group of friends.

Again, being an extrovert is not better than being an introvert. In the USA, society tends to value extroverts more than introverts so it is assumed that the former is better. That's not true. Your child can be a fabulous, successful, loving adult either way.

#20 – How do I help my child who is prone to mood swings?

I talked about brain development and hormonal surges above and I want to emphasize that **there may be more going on**. Mood swings, particularly in girls because of the onset or newness of their menstrual cycles, are very common. (In fact, that's something I ask about when I hear that a girl is moody).

But what behaviors are you characterizing as "mood swings"? Are you talking about the nice vs. nasty swings? Are you talking about the "I love you!" vs. "You suck!" mood swings? Are you talking about the snuggling vs. grumbling swings?

Some of this is normal. If the moodiness you are talking about is accompanied by almost constant rudeness, this is unacceptable. There is no excuse for being rude. If you tolerate such behavior not only will it continue, but it will teach your son or daughter that there are times when it is OK to be rude and he/she will have a hard time switching gears when rudeness is self-destructive (which is almost all the time, but I'm thinking of situations like college or job interviews, meeting other parents, or talking to an adult whose assistance they may need).

Teens' moods often reflect some unrest in the family home. Without attaching blame or assuming guilt, take a close look at recent events in your family. As adults, we all bear the responsibility for our unhealthy or rocky family relationships. Strengthening your marital relationship (even with an ex) can do wonders for your children's moods.

Moodiness can also be a sign of something more serious. Don't assume that you child is just being a "typical teen." Many teens are lovely, friendly, contented individuals. Notice how often these dark moods come up, notice the degree of darkness or anxiety, and notice how long the moods last. Talk to your teen. Ask your son or daughter what is going on. If they shut down, don't be afraid to get vulnerable and honest and share with them that you really want to be a good parent and you want to help them or get them any help they may need.

If you aren't making any headway, consult a physician or other professional. Drug and alcohol use, remorse about sexual behavior, abusive relationships, confusion about sexual orientation, and chemical imbalances can contribute to moodiness and self-destruction.

chapter four
Different types of teens

#21 – How do I handle a bossy teen?

You want to consider where she/he got this behavior. There are some behaviors that can be traced to the behavior of significant adults in the family. This is not to accuse you or anyone else; rather it is important to take note of whom your teen is emulating. **That person has the best opportunity to teach your child!** If they can both look at their part and then unravel it as a team, they can both grow immeasurably.

Your child sees bossiness as a behavior for which there is significant reward. I was a bossy child and here was my thinking:

- If I'm bossy nobody can push me around.
- If I'm bossy then I don't have to wonder why I'm unpopular. It's because everyone else is stupid.
- I do get laughs, sometimes, from being bossy.
- Only worthwhile people will see through my bossiness to who I really am.
- Maybe I can force my parents to get me stuff I want.
- Maybe I can force my parents to pay more attention to me.
- Maybe then someone will teach me how to be a nice person because I'm not sure how to do that.

I would bet that your bossy tween or teen is thinking at least one of these thoughts. Bossiness comes from a place of deep feelings of inferiority and loneliness. If you are the one your teen is bossing around then there's probably a good deal of insecurity and self-doubt mixed in—the adult is supposed to be the one in charge, after all.

What needs to happen? An intervention that will allow your teen to uncover his or her feelings and resolve them. I would recommend a therapist who can help you and your child explore the payoff of being a bossy child and a victimized parent. For instance, were you yourself bossy as a child? Were you bullied?

If you are receiving reports from the school or from other parents about your child bullying others, (or being bullied for that matter), do not ignore these messages. Contact your child's school principal or counselor immediately. Please don't take this lightly – a child's future may be at stake.

#22 – How do I handle an aggressive teen?

If you are afraid of your child, afraid for your safety or the safety of others because of your teen's aggression, it is imperative that you talk to a professional. Coaching is not enough in this sort of situation. Call a physician, psychologist, even the police. If you feel in danger at any given moment, call 911 immediately. *Calling the authorities does not mean that you don't love your child or that you are a bad parent.* You must take care of yourself and allow those with training to deal with your child.

#23 – How do I handle a needy or clingy teen?

Here are three reasons that a teen could be needy or clingy. If you notice your teen's clinging is lasting more than a month or so, I would recommend making an appointment with a physician or therapist. (If you sense that this can't wait a couple months, by all means, get help NOW).

1. **Your family has suffered a huge loss**—this could be the loss of a pet, relative, a parent's job, or your home. Moving away from a safe and thoroughly known environment can trigger fear and feelings of abandonment. Your teen is clinging because you are the apparent safety net in their environment. Since you probably share in this loss, take the lead in sharing your own feelings with your child but be careful not to share any of your own feelings of hopelessness, if you have them. This will scare your child immeasurably. Talk to him/her about how you are handling the loss. Perhaps creating a ritual to commemorate the person, place, or pet would be appropriate. People handle loss in different ways. There isn't one correct way —honor your teen's process and support him/her through it.

2. **Your teen has phobias.** These could be a phobia about school, about leaving the house, about appearance, about dogs in the neighborhood. Really, it could be anything. It may be that your child is being threatened by a bully or a group of bullies. Talk to your child and encourage him/her to share his/her feelings. **Above all, don't judge them.** If teens even SUSPECT that you are negatively judging them, they will shut down.

3. **Kids pick up on their parents' feelings of loss or abandonment**

and may become clingy as a way to support or protect YOU! While this is sweet and endearing, it is also unhealthy as it casts the child as the adult— the protector and nurturer of the parent. If you have suffered the loss of a relative, your marriage, your health, or something of significant monetary value, your child may be taking on this Protector role. Thank your child for his/her care and attention and assure them that, though you are sad and somewhat confused or frustrated, you have all the resources you need to get through this difficult time.

If you don't have all of those resources, I encourage you to connect with people who can make good referrals.

#24 – How do I handle a teen who likes to shock people with outrageous behavior?

Liking to shock people is a cry for attention. It happens when children **feel** they don't get enough attention. They feel they don't fit in with most people and this is their awkward attempt to affirm their self-worth. Look at your teen's actions and assess whether these actions are genuinely frightening or if he/she is simply displaying "odd" behavior compared to the rest of the family.

Shocking behavior that is frightening would be cutting, dressing provocatively, excessive piercing and tattooing, habitually breaking curfew, drug or alcohol experimentation, repeated or indiscriminate sexual activity, or getting into other illegal activities such as joyriding, theft, or tagging, to name several. Outrageous hair dying and cutting or wearing ripped clothes are often shocking but not necessarily dangerous.

Of course, this completely depends on what is the norm for your family. If you are worried, consult a professional, talk to other parents, or call the school and request an appointment with your teen's counselor. These are people who have a very good idea about what is "normal."

If your child is cutting or has unexplained bruises, it's time to get help from a physician or psychotherapist.

#25 – How do I handle a stubborn teen?

People are stubborn when they are afraid that they won't get what they think they need or that they'll lose something they have that they think they can't live without.

Teens tend to be stubborn because their brain chemistry makes just about everything seem important—either important to have or important not to have.

Whether they feel anxious because of their brain chemistry, a real situation, or both, reassurance and a strong yet loving presence works wonders. When a parent is wishy-washy, kids feel insecure. This is even true of children who are already young adults.

If your child is being stubborn about following house rules you can do several things. First, reflect on whether your rule makes sense TO YOU and whether it is in the best interest of your child. Sometimes we get tired and cranky ourselves and we make rules out of frustration or just to spite our kids. It's understandable but not fair, so take another look at your rules.

If you've decided that your rules are good rules, and your teen is still stubbornly ignoring them, give them a chance to change their minds—maybe a couple minutes, maybe a week, depending on what it is. If they don't change their minds, they get to live with the consequences. (And make sure you do have consequences!)

Another tactic is to budge a bit and give them a choice between two options. Make sure these are options that you can live with. Be careful, however, if your teen is particularly manipulative and you are particularly susceptible to his/her manipulations!

At the end of the day, you are the parent and you get to set the rules. It is completely legitimate to expect compliance with those rules.

#26 - How do I handle a dishonest teen?

Sometimes teens lie because they're embarrassed about something that happened. Sometimes they lie because they feel that they aren't enough just the way they are (That was my unconscious reason). Sometimes teens lie so that they can have a part of their lives that is theirs alone. Sometimes they lie to assert themselves as separate from their parents. Sometimes they lie because they have something to hide... Does your teen truly understand why lying is wrong? Do you?

I had a client whose ADD daughter lied constantly. I told the mother this is not uncommon for children with ADD but that the mother had to give her consequences. (This daughter actually lied so that her mother would step up and BE THE MOM!) Two months later the mother called and said, "She's still lying." When I asked what she had done in response she said she didn't think it was fair to punish a child for having ADD.

When you give consequences to your kids, you're not denying any physical, mental or emotional challenges that they might have but you're not excusing them either. We can't excuse bad behavior because they "can't help it." We must double our efforts to teach them how to live and thrive in harmony with our community.

chapter five
Teens at school

#27 – How do I handle lazy teens?

I don't believe in "lazy," because it's *always* something else. It could be depression, ADD/ADHD, a learning disability, lack of sleep, the need for attention, the need for more structure, and more. Calling kids "lazy," even thinking that they're lazy, sets them up for more of the same. When someone is lazy, his or her answer can always be "I don't know." A lazy person isn't expected to be responsible, so why try?

Assume that your children can be responsible. See them as responsible, talk to them as if they're responsible, give them some responsibility and hold them accountable for their actions. Then watch what happens; you will get a better idea about what's going on and they will not have "lazy" as an excuse to retreat from the family or their schoolwork. The school staff would be happy to team up with you, and teachers often have interesting and important insights since they are with your children almost every day.

#28 – How do I handle a gifted teen that is getting low grades?
A great many gifted kids have ADD/ADHD, but I'll tackle that in the next question.

Being gifted is often tough. Some kids just delight in their gifts. They're rather happy go lucky and enjoy just being themselves. Others (and these are the kids I see, so to me, they're the norm!) are confused or frustrated by the label.

Imagine—how can you ever live up to those expectations? Almost by definition you have to underachieve because anything less than excellence is considered underachieving. Gifted kids aren't allowed to have off days—someone or some internal voice is always asking "Why? What happened?"

So, a lot of times, gifted teens underachieve to relieve the pressure or to force the powers that be to take the label off. After all, it's often the parents that are the only ones getting pleasure out of their child's giftedness. If the label's off, there's less work, too!

Others underachieve because they're bored. Some teachers don't value divergent thinking; some teachers do value it, but they don't know how to make allowances for the student that requires a different set of expectations and grading. That's not taught in Teacher Training Programs!

What to do?

I firmly believe that it is not ONLY the school's responsibility to support the gifted student (in fact, some gifts aren't academic at all). If you had a child with a disability you would spend extra time and money to make sure that he/she was supported as much as possible so that he/she could be as successful as possible.

It's the same with a gifted child: they often require more time and more money to keep them stimulated and growing. But this can be super fun too! You get to take them all over the place – checking out fossils, listening to Beethoven, enjoying lectures about Surrealism, botulism, and Confucianism. How great is that?

Gifted kids need stimulation. You may have to request that they be allowed to do their own "special projects" during class time. You may have to request that they be allowed independent study time, apart from class time. Gifted teen athletes are allowed to miss physical education because they're up at 5:00 A.M. training for the Olympics. Perhaps your child's school could arrange something similar for your child's unique gift?

And last, but definitely not least, your gifted teen needs the same (if not more) boundaries and consequences as any other child. Teachers and parents often give gifted teens a lot of "wiggle room." I don't agree with this. I believe that gifted kids are more sensitive to the world and so need that sense of structure even more than non-gifted kids. I have seen so many of these kids get away with "murder" because the teacher or parent didn't want to believe that they were cheating on a test or ditching class, or they gave them yet one more chance to offer an empty apology. This doesn't work!

You can use the same loving boundaries for these kids. It actually brings relief from the pressures of the day because it's one thing they don't have to think about – the thinking is done for them when you create and uphold your rules and consequences. Their only decision is, "Do I feel like being punished today?" ☺

#29 – How can I help my ADD teen do better in school?

Here are 5 things you can do THIS WEEK to help your ADD child improve in school:

> 1. Give him/her more structure at home. Be present with your teen without hovering. Your teen is not yet responsible enough to regulate his/her studying time. You will need to sacrifice some of your free time so that you can be with him/her during homework time. For instance, you could sit in the room and read a

book, periodically checking on his/her progress.

2. Rewards. ADD kids respond to rewards because they also provide structure. "If I do X, Y will happen." This makes it much easier to accept the task. Don't go overboard with the reward though. Here are some examples of effective, yet easy to implement rewards. See which ones work for your family:

- Your child gets to pick the next night's dinner
- He/she gets to stay up an extra ½ hour
- You will take the trash out for him/her
- He/she gets the front seat for the next week
- He/she gets to purchase a song on iTunes

3. Keep in contact with your teen's teachers and counselors. Tell them you want to help them help your child. Ask them what you can do to make their jobs easier. Most teachers would **swoon** at the thought of a parent who wants to support the teacher's efforts. If your child has an IEP or 504 plan, make sure that you're upholding YOUR part of the contract. These are legal documents and they're as binding for you as they are for school personnel.

4. Find your child as much organic food as possible. If you go online and check out the effects of organic food

on behavior you will find that many prisons and continuation high school cafeterias have switched to organic food to calm their inmates/students. I've also read that if your child has the type of ADD characterized by angry outbursts feed him/her more whole grains. If he/she has Inattentive ADD, feed him/her more protein.

5. Aerobic exercise will stimulate the body's immune response and keep all systems running at optimal levels. It also encourages healthy brain function.

#30 – What do I tell my kids about cliques?

A clique is a large group of people who bond together over a common interest or outlook, often to the exclusion of others. In middle school/junior high and high school these groups can be mean; other times their exclusivity is perceived as arrogance when it isn't.

Drama cliques, choir cliques, band cliques, future business-leaders cliques and the like are generally not condescending to "outsiders," but they may take themselves so seriously that they simply are not interested in people who don't share their passion.

The arrogant cliques are the ones that are harder to explain away. The best thing you can do is encourage your teen's interests and applaud his/her efforts so that not belonging to a particular group is not such a hardship. They can be content with their own friends and their own particular way of doing things.

If cliques are a problem at your child's school, it's time to get the parents and the staff involved. Put "Cliques" on the agenda for your next Parent Association meeting. Check on the Internet for an expert in your area who can speak to the issue, and invite the counselors and the administration to help you understand the extent of the problem at your school. Craft an action plan for change. Volunteer to be on a task force to effect sweeping changes in this area—sort of a no-tolerance policy. It is people like you who change the world. ☺

#31 – What do I tell my kids about bullying?

Is your child the bully or the one being bullied?

At the risk of sounding harsh, **if you are receiving calls that your teen is bullying others, it's time to take him/her to a physician to initiate a medical evaluation.** By this age, teens know that bullying is wrong. There may be a physical or psychological reason why he/she needs to hurt people who are helpless and/or afraid. Bullies get a charge from seeing people cringe and cry. This is not an appropriate response. Please pursue some sort of medical or psychological support for your child.

Researcher Dan Olweus (see below) defines bullying as when a person is exposed "repeatedly and over time to negative actions on the part of one or more other persons." Negative action is defined as "when a person intentionally inflicts injury or discomfort upon another person through physical contact, through words, or in other ways."

If your child is being bullied there are a few of things that you can do; they require your time and persistence.

1. Talk to your child. Make sure he/she is OK. This may seem impossible for you to imagine, but all the school shooters in the United States were kids who said they were bullied.

Telling your child to "toughen up" is counterproductive. Some of the kids being bullied are kids who are too sensitive to deal with the "commotion" of confronting bullies. Being bullied is not a reflection on your child – it's about the bully. Focus on preventing perpetrators from continuing their behavior, rather than trying to toughen up the victims.

2. Talk to the school administration and the counselors. Talk to them again. Talk to them yet again. There should be a no-tolerance policy at schools. If they still won't listen, go to the school board and the district. This won't make you popular but bullying must not be ignored.

3. If there's still no response, organize the parents. Go to your school's parenting organization, go to the District, go to the School Board, go to the newspapers!

Bullying has become a huge problem and it is surprising how many school officials don't even understand the definition and excuse bad behavior, saying, "Kids have been teasing each other for hundreds of years. You/Your child are overreacting." ARRRRGH!

Here are some EXCELLENT resources:

- *The Bully, the bullied, and the bystander: From pre-school to high school – how parents and teachers can help break the cycle of violence.* By Barbara Coloroso.
- www.StopBullyingNow.com
- www.WordsCanHeal.org

- www.KidsAreWorthIt.com
- www.hazelden.org/web/go/olweusparent

#32 – What do I do if one of my kid's teachers hates him/her?

As a former teacher and school counselor I have to say that this rarely happens compared to how many times students *think* it's happening. What is more likely is that your child's teacher is very focused on the day's agenda and may forget or not have time to give your child the attention that he or she requires.

When we sit at a desk and look at the teacher it is a very different view than when we are up front teaching. A teacher sees the whole room—the 30+ students, the walls, the books, his or her own desk, the clock, the people passing by the windows—and needs to take it all in many times during a class period. Honestly, teachers just don't have time to "hate" a student.

If your child is acting up in class it is difficult to work and the teacher may speak sharply to your son or daughter. In fact, it is the student's **misbehavior** that the teacher hates because it often sets off the whole class. You know how hard it is to handle 1 or 2 kids who are acting up. Imagine having to handle 5, 6, 7, 35 ….

I would urge you to visit the classroom and see just how intricate is the "choreography" of any given class period. Watch your son or daughter and notice what role he or she plays. Is he/she making it smoother, not helping one way or another, or making his/her presence known with minor or major distractions? Make an appointment to talk to the teacher before and after your visit. If you still feel that the teacher is being unfair, arrange for a meeting with the teacher, the school principal, your child, and his or her counselor. This way, everybody will be supported and you will have the luxury of multiple viewpoints.

chapter six
Teens & relationships

#33 – What do I tell my tween or teen about being popular?

I have so many questions: How do you define "popular"? Were *you* popular when you were in high school? Does your child have friends at all? I'll pretend those are the questions I was asked and I'm pretty sure your answer will be in there. ☺

If by "popular" you mean "well liked," then you can support your children by teaching them social skills like sharing, being polite, being helpful, being a good listener, and being respectful. At the same time, teach them about being true to themselves; you don't want people to take advantage of their good natures.

If by "popular" you mean "Big Man on Campus," "Head Cheerleader," "Student Body President," I would say that you are overreaching and that this may be more about *you* than about your son/daughter. Which brings me to the second question: *Were you popular in high school?* Whether you were or weren't it is important to understand that popularity is not necessary for a person to be happy. Plenty of people are happy with a small yet strong group of devoted friends. Take an honest look at yourself – on the face of it, it seems you are imposing your needs, or even fears, on your child.

My third question is: Does your child have any friends at all? Maybe I'm naïve here, but in all my years working with teens I've met very few who didn't seem to have any friends. Studies show that as long as a child has ONE friend it's OK. Three is the average—some have one, some have five. It is very hard to find a child who doesn't have friends so if it is true that your son or daughter doesn't have any, I would guess that his or her social skills are very low. Even I, who was fairly irritating and socially inept up until college, had a group of friends. Was I popular in high school? No, but I was friendly with the head cheerleader and a few athletes and a student body officer or two. I was unhappy on all kinds of levels during my adolescence but I didn't stress about not having enough friends or the right kind of friends.

I would suggest involving your teen in some casual group activities in combination with therapy or coaching. This would help your child learn to read and understand other people while practicing his/her social skills in a setting that doesn't demand excellence. Church or similar youth groups are great for this since they teach tolerance and friendliness.

#34 – What do I tell my kids about peer pressure?

What I've learned from working at schools is that there are SO MANY distractions that it's hard to think and hard to decide what to do. Why not just choose what everyone else is doing? That's why having a strong family is so important. Your voice needs to be bigger than the voices of hundreds of teens.

Peer pressure makes individuals seek to create conformity or agree to conform in order to fit in or be accepted. The truth is that adults succumb to peer pressure too, so you can use your own experience to talk to your kids about why we feel the need to belong and how to create healthy peer groups. Whenever peer pressure or the need to belong informs our decisions we are not being true to ourselves. Teens are big on being themselves, expressing their identities, and not having their individuality squelched. You can talk to your teen about your own experiences with these and create scenarios to illustrate how peer pressure can kill your ability to be your own person. Your teen may need to engage in more esteem-building activities so that they are reminded of their strengths and can focus on them.

#35 – My 13-year old is 47 mentally and 10 emotionally. He/she has a very hard time making and keeping friends. What can I do to help?

Watching a terrific kid struggle socially is painful. I have worked with so many teens that just don't seem to fit in: their interests are more sophisticated and/or their social skills are very underdeveloped.

Try this slow and gentle process to support your misunderstood teen:

1) Compile a list of personal strengths or positive personality traits.

2) Go over the list with your child and choose 3 of his/her most outstanding traits.

3) Discuss how these traits show themselves in day-to-day life.

4) Create an action plan of 1 or 2 ways to strengthen each trait.

5) Make an agreement to notice and praise when your child is displaying those strengths. In turn, your child tells you when those traits showed up during his/her day.

6) Take time to discuss how these traits are beneficial to people and how your teen can start to

incorporate them into his/her interactions with others.

7) Continue to reassure, to point out strengths and to discuss them, but now do the same process with one or two of your child's "less charming" traits. Perhaps he/she interrupts a lot, corrects other people, sulks, tells incomprehensible jokes, is judgmental, self-centered, or shy. You know your child and you know which traits will be easiest to work with. Start there.

What is also helpful is to point out and discuss inappropriate or unappreciated behavior in fictional characters. This may make it easier for your child to see and to discuss his/her own behavior.

#36 – How do I get my son/daughter out of an abusive relationship?

This is tricky, isn't it? Abuse can come out of nowhere and often our teens just can't see what's going on. They think it's just a form of love and that all their friend needs is kindness and understanding. Those are such good intentions but our kids aren't trained to be therapists for each other. The sort of kindness and understanding that an abuser needs is offered by a trained professional.

When you forbid children to see particular friends, they often redouble their efforts, so that's not always the best scenario. Again, this depends on the severity of the abuse. Talk to your son/daughter and see if you can gather some information. Talk to your teen's counselor to find out if this friend is a serious threat (a call-the-police-and-get-a-restraining-order threat).

I had a client (a multi-gifted teen who was usually very mature emotionally) whose boyfriend was just being a jerk to her. He wasn't as polite as he could be and he was pretty self-centered. During our sessions I talked to her about how real men treat the people they love. She felt that praying for him would change him. I suggested that she pray for him, but let God change him! Eventually she got bored with him. Years later, she is now married to a wonderful man.

I had a male student one year who had it all: brains, good looks, lots of friends, a killer tennis swing, and a heck of a future ahead of him. His girlfriend was in my class too and most of the time they got along well. But sometimes, out of nowhere, she would nag him about something very insignificant. (She actually sounded like a nagging mom!) I don't know why he stayed with her with all that criticism. Sometimes, when I would have the kids doing group work, I would put him in a group with a couple of really sweet girls, just so he could experience the difference!

Sometimes we attract abusers into our lives because we're accustomed to that kind of treatment. Is there or has there been abuse in your home? If so, this is a great opportunity to talk to your teen about how you learned to handle abusive situations.

When abuse is extreme and relentless, it indicates that both parties have some underdeveloped social skills. It's important to get some support to help your child. These things have a way of repeating themselves—same person, different body – if the pattern isn't broken.

#37 – Do I have to talk to my teen about sex? Don't they know everything by now?

Yes you do. BUT... how about looking at it this way— the Sex Talk is really a talk about how to be a man or woman with self-respect and dignity. It's about what it takes to be a best friend. Focus on that but don't shy away from talking about sex and pregnancy and STDs and birth control. This is important information, no matter what your moral stance is. (The statistics on teen pregnancy and teens with sexually transmitted diseases are horrifying).

If you have strong religious beliefs that inform your position on pre-marital sex, by all means, pepper your talk with that information, but know that kids engage in sexual activity for all sorts of reasons including revenge, loneliness, and shame.

It should be an on-going conversation; you never know when your child will come up with some idea about why NOW it's time to have sex. (I went to grad school with a girl from a religious upbringing, who had sex with her high school boyfriend because he was depressed and she thought that might help. It didn't. He killed himself.) What a horrible thing for both those young people to go through.

If you don't have a religion on which to base your beliefs about teens and sex, you may need to take the "what mature adults do" approach. In our society we see so many adults having immature sexual relationships that kids think that's the norm. But mature adults generally do not have one-night stands. They wait. They learn to trust themselves and then they learn whether or not they can trust their friend. They get tested, as a couple; they use birth control, they are friends first and lovers second.

In teen relationships, sex is often used as a loyalty test. That is manipulative and underhanded. It's a lie to talk about loyalty and losing one's virginity in the same sentence. It's a lie for a young person to talk about true love and have a secret half-naked rendezvous in the school bathroom or the back seat of a car.

Teach your children about the wonder and majesty of love and, if you haven't experienced that, find someone that you and your teen trust to help with those conversations.

Amy Lang of Birds+Bees+Kids® recommends the following titles to help with your talks:

- **It's Perfectly Normal** by Robie Harris (Ages 10 and up)
- **What Hollywood Won't Tell You About Sex, Love and Dating** by Greg Johnson and Susie Shellenberger (Ages 12 and up)
- **Changing Bodies, Changing Lives** by Ruth Bell (Ages 13, 14 and up)

#38 – How do I get my daughter to stop talking about her sexual adventures?

Is she talking to you because she wants guidance or because she wants to drive you crazy?
If it's the former, keep listening. Sometimes kids talk about sex so they can have permission to NOT have sex. She trusts you and that's a good thing. Keep the channels open.

If she's just trying to bug you, it's time for you to take over the conversation: start asking about getting tested, about STDs, about birth control, about getting pregnant and about having to put all her dreams on hold while she raises a baby...alone. (Because you're not going to give up YOUR life too, are you?) Take her to a doctor. Make sure she's OK. You're the parent; take control again.

chapter seven
New partner, new marriage

#39 – How do I get my teen to accept my dating again?

A bunch of interesting things happen to your teens when you start dating again. Here's a list:

- Guys want to protect their mothers but are also sort of happy for their fathers;
- Girls are often OK with their mothers dating as long as they have a crush on the new boyfriend. Otherwise they worry that he'll take mom away;
- They start imagining you having sex – Ewwww;
- If they don't have their own friend, they start feeling a bit inadequate;
- They feel betrayed;
- They think you're selfish;
- They worry about being abandoned;
- They wonder why you get to have fun when they're still in pain about the divorce;
- They wonder if you ever really loved their other parent – you know, the one you partnered with to create your kids in the first place.

And more...

Some have all these thoughts and some have one or two.

So how are you going to get some acceptance? By making sure that you are paying attention to them, talking to them about your dating (the everyday creating-a-bond positive part, not the part about how immature you feel or the sex part), and spending time letting them talk to you about all these scary and embarrassing thoughts.

And if your children don't like the person you're dating, don't ignore that. Find a way to talk it through, by yourselves or with a therapist or coach. They may be wrong about what they THINK about your new friend, but they're allowed to FEEL their feelings. Those are never wrong. Honor that and you've done a lot to begin whatever healing needs to be done.

#40 – Why does my teen keep saying that I've BETRAYED him/her?

This is so common I almost expect it. Keep in mind that teens are not as facile and flexible with their emotions as you might be. First you tell them that everything they've counted on (in their opinion) is irreparably damaged. Next you tell them to get used to their new lives. Then, once they've started to get used to this new life, you bring another person in. WHAT? What about everything you said? You said you wouldn't get married until X happened! You said you wouldn't date until Y happened! You said that YOU and I were going to do Z— how come SHE/HE is coming along!

Disloyalty – whether real or perceived - is EXCRUCIATING for teens; make no mistake!

In a very real sense, you HAVE betrayed your son or daughter. Why not accept it and apologize and tell them why the rules have changed. (And it better be for a good reason if you want any kind of respect!) And then carry on with your life, understanding that betrayal takes a while to get over and that they need you a lot now for reassurance and stability.

It's okay to have a love life. It's not okay to gloss over it when it affects your children.

#41 – How do I get my teens to accept my upcoming marriage?

Just as their sexuality is budding, you have to go and get yourself your own lover. EW. Not a pretty picture for most teens. Your kids may be jealous, hurt, confused, angry and/or disgusted. They may try to sabotage your happiness by picking fights or creating drama.

Here are 3 do's:
- Get your kids' input about anything that will directly affect them (like moving, changing schools, sharing a bedroom). Really hear what they're saying and try to find a compromise. After all, the way they see it, you're getting all the benefits and just leaving them high and dry.

- Talk about how much and why you love your new spouse. Let them see and feel the love and joy in your heart, without diminishing or putting down your former spouse (their parent).

- Thank them every time they are willing to be accommodating. This is a big deal for them and requires quite a bit of maturity. And tell them how much you love them!

Here are 3 don'ts:
- Don't be super physical with your partner in front of them. There's

time enough for them to get used to you being all lovey-dovey. A kiss hello and goodbye is fine but, for instance, if you are snuggling with your new honey while the whole family is watching a DVD, they will probably be uncomfortable. Be the mature ones. It will make things easier!

- Don't compare your new honey to their other parent—BIG NO-NO! Just don't do it. Say nice things about both of them.

- Don't let your kids nag you into feeling guilty about loving someone new. Sometimes kids think that if they bug you enough you'll relent and break up with your future spouse. Stop that behavior in its tracks.

#42 – How do I prepare my kids for a new stepparent?

Here's my biggest piece of advice: as soon as possible set up regular meetings between you, your ex, and any current or future spouses or partners so that all are involved and on the same page regarding the rules and consequences in your family. You are still a family, even with additional players. **Leaving out the stepparents or co-parents is insulting and teaches your children that they don't have to respect the new members.** That is a recipe for disaster. (see question #44)

Then have a whole family meeting and let your kids know what the rules are and that everyone is going to follow them. Reassure them that your new spouse is not going to come in and make his/her own rules, that all the adults have come together to create the same structure AND that your new spouse is another adult in the family and, as such, is allowed to follow through on consequences. Keep the love flowing and assure them that, though you understand that change is difficult, it is all for the purpose of creating a happier, stronger family.

If this kind of extended family arrangement isn't possible because of your relationship with your ex, check out the next question.

#43 – What are your Top 5 parenting tips for new stepparents?

1. Don't compare your kids (or other kids if you aren't a parent yet) to your new spouse's kids. That is a recipe for misery. When we resist reality we create many more problems than when we accept what is and work with that.

2. Don't worry about them liking you. Teens are like dogs sniffing out the competition. As long as they are not rude to you, you're good.

3. Don't take things personally. Divorce is a painful, painful process whose effects often last longer for the kids than for the parents.

4. Love them as much as you can and don't be afraid to make your love grow. Be loving to them without expecting anything in return. You soften your image, you soften the situation, and you teach them how to

be unselfish about love. What a lesson!

5. Look for the little triumphs. Remember that teens don't always trust easily. If they're talking to you, that is HUGE! There's plenty of time to enjoy the big triumphs. I still remember the first time my stepson introduced me as his stepmother. It was so exciting I didn't want to breathe because I thought he might take it back! I still get a thrill when he calls me his stepmother and he turns 30 this year!

#44 – We have a blended family with 5 kids of various ages. All have adjusted well and get along well, except one. What do we do about her? She's trying our patience.

First of all, congratulations on having a fairly smooth transition. That's wonderful! Families are interesting. Sometimes we'll see two extroverted parents and they'll have an introverted child. Sometimes the whole family tends toward domesticity – a warmth and calm closeness that is in stark contrast to the ADHD child who wants to run around and yell all day. Sometimes we find one delicate child living among a rough and tumble group. These situations can really be confusing.

It's easy to put the blame or responsibility for this confusion on the "odd" child. As one prospective client said to me, "There are three of us in this house who are all the same, and there is one who is different. He is the one creating unhappiness in our family."

In your situation I would guess that the daughter you speak of is very **sensitive**.

Sensitive kids perceive the world quite differently than other folks.

Here are 3 main differences:

1. **Everything feels significant.** Sensitive people feel EVERYTHING so there's no way for them to naturally or instinctively sift out what may be a superficial issue.

2. **Everything feels real.** Sensitive people feel deeply and because of this, it all seems real. How can they experience such a profound (and painful) emotion and it NOT be real?

3. **Sensitive people are not *naturally* fun-loving.** Sure, they have moments that are fun, moments when they laugh, but they are not naturals at creating fun.

Sensitive people need to be guided through the day-to-day human experience much more than others do.

This in no way suggests that they are less intelligent or less capable. If your child had a broken leg, you wouldn't think that they are less capable of walking, just that something is in the way temporarily and he/she needs a crutch. Sensitive people are perfectly capable of having happy, productive, fulfilling lives, once they have been shown how to maneuver through the **swamp** of everyday life!

Realizing that your child is sensitive will help you to be kinder and gentler to them. They need and put a high value on lots of love, reassurance and attention. And they need those things to be presented in a way that is comfortable FOR THEM (not necessarily for you). Some sensitive kids love to be held, some aren't so keen on physical contact. Some learn better through conversation, some through literature, others through TV.

Talk to your child and, more importantly, LISTEN to what they have to say. Don't be afraid of their answers. They will tell you what they need if you let them know that you care to hear it. It may take some practice, but it will be worth your time and attention. Also, go back to some of the earlier suggestions in this book – these will help you communicate with your child.

Remember that "sensitive" does not equal "crippled;" it just means that they need a crutch for now.

#45 – Why is co-parenting so important?

Quite simply, when a child's world is turned upside down, the most powerful thing anyone can do is to create a unified coalition of responsible, loving adults whose goal is to strengthen the family. Co-parenting is when ALL—or nearly all—of the significant adults in a child's immediate world come together to establish and maintain the structure of that child's life by discussing issues as a group.

For example, they might discuss which extracurricular activities the child is involved in, given his or her interests of course. They may discuss car purchasing, vacations, and bed times. They would certainly discuss and come to an agreement about rules and consequences. There would be no secrets or surprises, no "one-upping" each other. When parents are willing to put in the time and energy to come together to create a stable environment for their kids, the result is amazing! It gives the child a sense of security and a knowing that he or she is loved and cared for by all the adults in his or her family. I cannot recommend this highly enough.

conclusion – what's next?

Parenting has so much shame attached to it:

- Am I doing this right?
- Why isn't my child better behaved?
- Why is it so hard?
- Why do I feel like quitting?
- I'm such a bad parent!
- Can everyone tell that our home isn't happy?
- I swore I wouldn't parent like *my* parents and now, here I am, saying the things THEY used to say!
- I'm not parenting like my parents – why isn't it working?

And yet, here you are, reaching out for guidance. That's HEROIC in my book.

If you've seen epic films like **Star Wars** or **Lord of the Rings** or even **Princess Diaries** (!) you know that the hero accepts the challenge to bring order and restore goodness by defeating evil (even if "evil" is a bunch of gum-snapping snobby girls!).

You also know that at some point, the hero wants to turn back, feeling incapable of the task at hand. **This resistance is part of the pattern.** You may experience resistance from your kids or *from yourself.* That's not a bad thing; **it ALWAYS happens.** If it happens to you, that doesn't make you less of a hero, it makes you MORE OF A HERO!

And at that point, a soothing presence appears to inspire the hero to complete the task and restore balance.

If this book serves as that soothing presence, I am honored. If you feel that you want a more personal touch, I invite you to give me a call: **206-326-8446** or send me an email: Margit@TheGiftedTeenCoach.com.

It's always a privilege to serve a dedicated parent!

about margit crane:

Margit Crane, M.A., M.S., M.Ed., is The Gifted-Teen Coach. She is a speaker, author, workshop leader and acclaimed child development, family relationship, and learning specialist.

A middle and high school teacher for twenty-five years, Margit has coached thousands of teens and parents to achieve greater sanity, deeper love and respect, clearer communication, and a lot more FUN in their relationships with family and friends.

Margit specializes in coaching gifted tweens and teens who are under-achieving, over-irritating, or both! Often diagnosed with ADD/ADHD, these high-spirited kids are misunderstood and disregarded, all of which affect family harmony, personal esteem and confidence.

Margit's coaching and the techniques she employs are tailored for the individual client and family. All her coaching packages – whether phone or in-person - are designed to provide maximum results.

***For more information** about other parenting tools, speaking opportunities, workshops, teleclasses, OR to inquire about booking a coaching session, call 206-326-8446 or go to www.TheGiftedTeenCoach.com or www.MargitCrane.com.

Made in the USA
Lexington, KY
03 December 2010